DI

ROBLOX
BACON HAIR BOY

Books 1-3

Respawn Press

www.RespawnPress.com

Published by Respawn Press,
an imprint of Sparkwell Publishing.
www.RespawnPress.com

Paperback ISBN: 978-1-960927-06-4

Thank You!

Thank you for purchasing a copy of this book!

If you like it and would like to read more books featuring Billy Blox and his friends, please leave a review on Amazon or Goodreads.

Get a Free Ebook

Visit RespawnPress.com to download a **free short story** and printable activity pages.

Join our Roblox Group

Our Roblox group has **300+ members**! Join to ask the author questions and to meet other fans of the books. Simply search "Arrikin Books" in the Roblox group search.

Fan Mail

Send fan mail to this email: books@arrikin.com. **Please ask your parents for permission before sending fan mail**.

To view fan art by other fans, visit:

arrikinbooks.com/fan-creations

Contents

DIARY OF A
ROBLOX
BACON HAIR BOY

Book 1: New School

Respawn Press

www.RespawnPress.com

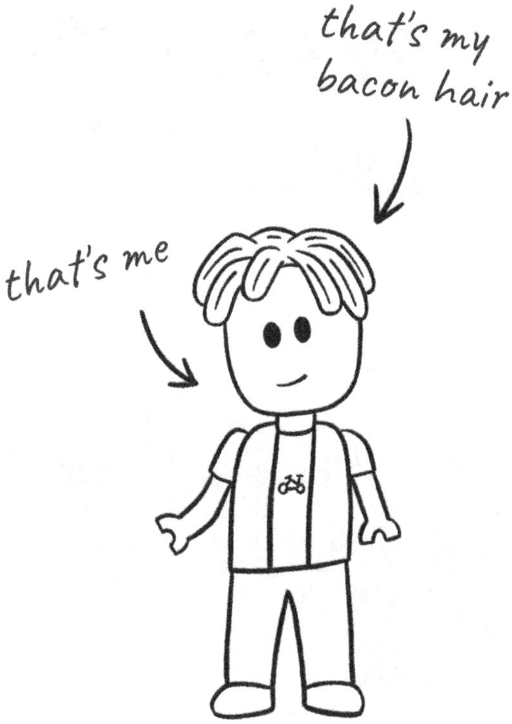
that's my
bacon hair
that's me

Monday

"Billy, it's time to get up," my mom whispered.

I kept my eyes closed and pretended not to hear her.

I hoped she would give up and let me sleep more.

She gently tapped my shoulder.

"It's time to get ready for school," she whispered.

I stopped pretending to be asleep and got up to get dressed.

Today was my first day at a new school, so I was nervous.

I told my mom I was worried my new teachers and classmates wouldn't like me.

I told her I would miss my friends.

She told me to write in this ~~diary~~ journal every day so that by the end of my first week, I could go back and read how silly I was.

She said I would have plenty of new friends by the end of the week.

I was right to be nervous.

Everybody in the school hallways turned to stare at me while I walked by.

I don't think they've seen many bacon hairs before.

I walked into my classroom and sat at an

empty desk.

I closed my eyes and pretended I was back at my old school, where all my friends had bacon hair. Nobody looked at me weirdly there.

But here, even the teacher looked at me weirdly.

"Are you new to this school?" someone behind me asked.

I turned around and saw the prettiest girl I have ever seen.

She was sitting at the desk behind me.

She was wearing a white pearl necklace that matched her smile.

I told her it was my first day in this school and that it was much bigger than my old school.

She smiled and asked for my name.

I told her my name is Billy Blox.

She was about to tell me her name, but our teacher asked us all to face forward. The lesson was about to begin.

Maybe this school isn't going to be so bad after all.

Tuesday

Today was not a very good day...

Three slenders came up to me while I grabbed my lunch at school.

All three of them had spiky hair and wore black clothes.

is that a bird nest?

Tom   Jay   Flinn

"What's your name, bacon boy?" one slender asked me.

I told him my name is Billy Blox and he rolled his eyes.

He told me his name was Jay and his two friends were Tom and Flinn.

I was about to tell them it was nice to meet them, but Jay interrupted me.

He said I shouldn't bother to remember their names because they don't talk to bacon hairs.

The three of them laughed and walked away.

My mom thinks this school is going to be good for me.

This school has more advanced classes than

my old one.

Some of the classes teach you how to make builds and write scripts.

She thinks I can make a lot of Robux one day when I'm older and I won't have to be a bacon hair anymore.

But I don't know. I would rather be an explorer instead.

There are many experiences that people haven't even seen yet. They are just waiting to be explored!

One time my best friend Jerry and I went to an experience called **Animal Simulator** where we could become animals.

I became a police penguin and Jerry became a cowboy penguin.

We went swimming in a small stream and

were having so much fun, but then someone who was a wolf started chasing us.

He was so much faster and had big, scary claws.

He kept **OOFing** us until we gave up and left the experience.

I bet it was a slender who turned into that wolf.

They are always so mean to us...

Wednesday

Today I discovered I'm not the only bacon hair boy in school!

My teacher asked me to go to the library to see if the book sale had started.

When I went into the library, I saw that another class was already looking at the books.

One of the boys in that class had bacon hair like me!

We saw each other and smiled but didn't say hi.

Sometimes I like to pretend that I'm not a

bacon hair and that other students aren't staring at me while I walk by.

I always try to stay quiet so others won't even notice I'm there...

I have bacon hair

he has bacon hair

same shirt??

My previous school used to have book sales too.

One time, Jerry and I bought a spy book.

The book cover had a big, green question mark.

The book came with a special pen that had invisible ink. You had to hold the paper up to the light in order to read the secret message.

Jerry and I used to exchange secret messages during class so the teacher couldn't see what we were talking about.

We used those messages to plan our weekends and to decide which experiences to visit.

I miss being in school with Jerry.

I still see him in the afternoons because teleporting to each other's houses is easy.

But I still miss having somebody to talk to at school.

Maybe I can find the bacon hair boy I saw today.

Maybe he has the same lunchtime as me.

I just hope Jerry doesn't get mad.

We have been best friends since we were little so he might get jealous.

Thursday

I couldn't find the other bacon hair boy at school today.

I looked everywhere during lunch but couldn't find him.

Maybe people are mean to him as well and he hides during lunch.

I wish I knew where he was hiding so that I could hide there too...

Later in the day, I was getting my stuff from my locker when I heard somebody say, "Bacon boy, when are you going to stop being a bacon hair? Don't you know this is a rich school?"

I turned around and saw the 3 slender boys from the other day... Jay, Tom, and Flinn.

They laughed when I told them I didn't have Robux to change my hair.

They told me I was embarrassing their school with my bacon hair.

"Don't you know how annoying it is to see your ugly bacon hair every day?" Jay asked.

I told them my mom only had enough Robux to pay for my school supplies and the house bills.

I told them there was nothing I could do about my hair.

But Jay said there was something I **COULD** do about it.

He turned to Tom and Flinn and told them

to toss me into my locker.

They both grabbed me and shoved me into my locker.

Jay slammed the locker door shut before I could get out.

"Finally, no more bacon hair," Jay said in between laughs.

I could hear their laughs get softer as they walked away.

imagine getting locked in there

I was too embarrassed to yell for help.

People would just think of me as the weird bacon hair boy.

I also didn't want my mom to get worried. She really likes this school.

So I did the only thing I could think of. I reset myself.

OOF.

I respawned at the school entrance and walked back inside as if nothing happened.

Friday

I saw something strange at school today.

The pretty girl from my class was talking to the slenders during lunch.

She was talking to them while they were in line to get food, but she didn't sit with them.

The slenders sat together at one table, and she sat with girls at a different one.

Maybe they're friends...

I haven't had a chance to ask her what her name is.

It turns out the desk I sat on during my first day of school belonged to another student who was absent that day.

The student came back the next day, so the teacher moved me to a different desk.

Since then I haven't been able to speak with the girl.

I wonder what experiences she likes to visit after school.

My friend Jerry and I are going to role-play in **Brookhaven** with our other friend George.

George is one of the few people at my old school who isn't a bacon hair.

George and his older brother learned how to design shirts when they were younger, so they were able to save Robux to buy new hair.

Even though George isn't a bacon hair

anymore, he is nice to other bacon hairs like me.

That's why Jerry and I like him.

George's cool hair

George's cool shirt

Saturday

Today my friends and I went to **Brookhaven** to role-play cops vs robbers.

Jerry was the cop. George and I were the fugitive robbers.

George and I went to hide in the car wash behind the Rotten Robbie gas station.

"Jerry told me some slender boys are bullying you at your new school," George said.

I told him that they locked me in my locker and I had to reset myself to get out.

"OOOF," he said.

"I know," I said.

I told him that everybody in my new school stares at me when they first see me.

He said to ignore them because they don't know any better.

He told me he is nice to bacon hairs because he used to be one, so he knows what it feels like when people make fun of you.

He said my new classmates are probably spoiled. He thinks they were never bacon hairs, so they don't know what it's like to be teased for not having Robux.

I kept an eye out for Jerry every now and then.

He was inside the Auto Shop on the opposite side of the gas station when I was talking to George.

George and I started talking about **Bedwars**

and what battle passes we would buy if we had a million Robux.

The three of us play **Bedwars** sometimes but some of the kits are OP and we can't beat them.

One time I saved enough Robux to buy the Eldertree kit.

I was able to win matches with the Eldertree kit, but it got nerfed a few weeks later.

If we buy more kits, we might be able to win more games.

Too bad we don't have more Robux.

While we were talking, I noticed that Jerry wasn't in the Auto Shop anymore.

"Hands up you two!"

We turned around and saw Jerry standing behind us.

He had entered the car wash from the back side.

"We haven't done anything wrong, officer!" George yelled.

"Tell that to the judge," Jerry said in a deep voice.

We played for a while longer and took turns being the cop and the robbers. It was a fun afternoon.

I think my new school wouldn't be so bad if George and Jerry were there with me.

Sunday

I had a very strange and scary dream last night.

I dreamed I was walking into school but all the lights were off.

The hallways were empty and everything was quiet.

There were backpacks and books on the floor as if people had just disappeared into thin air.

"Hello?" I asked in a loud whisper.

I wasn't sure if I should be loud or quiet.

What if something bad was going on?

I poked my head into several classrooms but I still couldn't find anyone.

The classrooms had empty desks and more books and backpacks on the floor.

Either people just disappeared or they ran out in a rush and left everything behind.

It was weird...

"Bacon boy!" someone yelled in the distance.

I turned and saw the slender boys walking toward me.

Their skin was green and their eyes were glowing red.

As they were getting closer, Flinn said they were hungry and wanted to eat my brain.

That's when I knew I had to run!

I turned and ran in the opposite direction toward one of the emergency exits.

I shoved the door open and ran outside but somehow I was back inside the school!

The slender boys were getting closer and closer.

I turned again and ran out the door. But I still appeared inside the school again.

It's like somebody had put an invisible portal that sends you back into the school.

I felt trapped with nowhere else to run. I didn't know what to do.

I ran out the door one more time and again I was back in school.

The slender boys were right in front of me this time.

They opened their mouths and showed me their sharp teeth.

I squeezed my eyes shut and slowly walked backward.

That's when I heard my mom's voice telling me it was time for breakfast.

She woke me up just in time!

Monday

I was nervous when I went to school today.

I looked around and everything appeared normal.

The lights were on and the students and teachers were all there.

It was just a normal day.

I went to my locker to grab my books for class when I heard a voice in the distance.

"Hey bacon boy!" the familiar voice yelled.

The voice sounded far but I knew they were probably walking toward me.

I turned in the direction of the yell.

I was expecting to see the slenders with green skin and red glowing eyes walking toward me.

But I didn't see them. They weren't there.

Then I heard the voice again. It was coming from down the hallway.

The three slenders were laughing and shoving a boy into a locker.

They high-fived each other and walked into a classroom.

I waited a bit to make sure they weren't coming back out into the hallway. When I was sure they were gone, I went to the locker where the boy was trapped.

"Hello?" I whispered into the locker.

A voice whispered back.

The boy asked if they had left and I told him that they had.

He told me his locker code and I used it to open the lock.

A bacon hair boy came out of the locker.

It was the same bacon hair boy I saw at the library the other day!

I asked him if he recognized me from the library and he said that he did.

I told him I was trying to look for him during lunch but couldn't find him.

He told me his name is Brock.

He said he likes to eat lunch outside, at the tables by the playground.

He eats with other bacon hair kids and said that I should join them tomorrow.

THERE ARE OTHER BACON HAIRS IN THIS SCHOOL???

Tuesday

I met up with Brock today at lunch.

He waited for me by the cafeteria entrance.

We got in line together and got our food.

I then followed him outside. I didn't even know we were allowed to eat outside!

There were a few outdoor tables with big, yellow umbrellas for shade.

We walked to the side of the cafeteria building and sat at a table where two other bacon hairs were eating.

He introduced me to them. The boy's name is Clay, and the girl's name is Sophia.

Clay waved hello. He was chomping down a slice of pizza. Sophia said hi.

Brock told them that the slenders had shoved him into his locker again and that I had helped him out.

"They did that to me too," I told them.

It turns out that the slenders bully all the bacon hair students in the school, not just me.

I also told them that nobody in class talks

to me.

"Do YOU talk to them?" Sophia asked.

I told her I didn't...

She said that most students in this school are nice to bacon hairs and that I should make an effort to talk to them.

I told her I was afraid they wouldn't like bacon hairs.

"You won't know until you talk to them," she said.

I asked them if they had any other friends who were not bacon hairs.

"Yes of course," Brock said.

Clay told me that they like to eat with other bacon hairs during lunch, but when they're in class they talk to other students.

He munched on his pizza while he talked.

He said that they even hang out with some of the other students after school.

"You're the new kid in school," Sophia said. "The other students don't know if you're nice or not. Just talk to them. If you're nice to them, they'll be nice to you."

I promised them I would talk to other students in my class.

Hopefully they are nice to me.

Wednesday

I talked to a boy in class today and it went well!

He was reading something on his tablet during our 5-minute class break.

I felt bad interrupting him, but Sophia was right. I had to talk to people to make friends.

I asked him what he was reading. He looked up at me and then back down at his tablet.

"I'm reading a scary story," he said.

I asked him if he had read Arrikin's scary Roblox stories.

He nodded his head. "I'm reading his new book," he said.

"Have you read the story where a boy finds a Roblox game that can grant wishes?" I asked him.

"That's my favorite story," he said.

I told him it was my favorite story too.

He stopped reading and looked up at me again.

He said Arrikin was turning the scary

Roblox stories into YouTube videos.

He said some of our classmates were watching them during class. But a few of them said they were too scary and couldn't finish watching them.

Apparently the videos had scary music and creepy sound effects that made them a lot scarier than the books.

I told the boy my name, and he introduced himself as Lucas.

He looked down at his tablet and started reading again.

I asked him what he likes to do after school.

He said he likes to draw but that he's not very good at it.

He mostly does it to please his strict

parents.

"They don't let me out much, so I keep myself busy with art," Lucas said.

"Why not?" I asked him.

I told him my mom lets me go to different experiences all the time.

He said that his little brother got lost once and now his parents are super strict and don't let them out much.

"Well... there is one place they let me visit sometimes," Lucas said.

He told me our classmates like to hang out at an arcade called Atlantis Arcade. They go there after school and on weekends.

If I want to make friends, I should go to the arcade soon!

Thursday

I decided that I am going to the arcade tomorrow.

The other bacon hair students told me even they go to the arcade sometimes!

The only problem is that I don't have many Robux to use in the arcade machines.

If I go and don't play games, people might think I'm poor and won't want to talk to me.

I think I can use my mom's credit card and use a few Robux to play some games.

I don't even have to play too many games or spend too many Robux.

As long as I play a few games, people will think I can afford it.

If I only spend a few Robux, my mom won't even know I used her card.

I know she keeps it in her purse and that she puts her purse on her nightstand during the day when she's home.

Before I go to the arcade tomorrow, I can sneak into her room and get the credit card from her purse.

it's like a treasure chest

Then when I get back, I can sneak into her room again and put the credit card back before she even notices it's gone.

And since I'll only use a few Robux, she won't even notice the difference in her bank account.

I talked to Lucas in class again today.

He told me the name of the pretty girl in our class.

Her name is Emily and she loves to go to the arcade!

But there's one problem...

Lucas said the slender boys also like to go to that arcade. A LOT.

I think that's why she was talking to them the other day.

They were probably planning to go to the arcade together.

If I'm going to play arcade games, I need to make sure I'm good. If I don't, they'll probably think I'm a loser and bully me even more!

Friday

I asked Brock to come to the arcade with me and he said yes.

He is going to stop by my house soon so we can go together.

I'll grab my mom's credit card as soon as Brock arrives. I don't want to get caught with the card before I even leave the house!

Okay, I'm going to get ready because he'll be here soon.

Wow, the arcade was so much fun!

As soon as Brock texted that he was outside, I sneaked into my mom's room and got her credit card.

I hid it in my back pocket, and then I went and told her I was leaving for the arcade.

We spawned at the entrance of the arcade and went inside.

The lights were dim and the patterns on the carpet were glowing in the dark.

The arcade games were flashing bright lights and buzzing with different sounds.

I saw a few classmates, but most of the people there were strangers.

I THINK they all go to my school but I'm not sure.

Brock and I seemed to be the only bacon

hair kids in the arcade but that didn't matter.

Nobody was looking at us weirdly. They were all busy playing their games.

At the very back of the arcade was a small room with a transparent glass wall.

There were chairs and tables in that room and vending machines with snacks and drinks.

Brock asked me if I had Robux for the games.

I told him I did and showed him my mom's credit card.

"Wow, you must have very nice parents!" he said.

We went and played a racing game where

you have to sit on a fake motorcycle to steer the motorcycle in the game.

Then we went and played a game where we had to use fake guns to shoot at the zombies on the screen.

I didn't get to see Emily at the arcade today, but I still had fun.

The good thing is that we didn't bump into any of the slenders either.

When I got back home, I sneaked into mom's room and put her card back in her purse.

I only used like 12 Robux so she's never going to notice.

I want to go back to the arcade tomorrow.

Hopefully, Emily will be there.

Saturday

Today I went to the arcade by myself.

I took my mom's credit card again and teleported into the arcade entrance.

When I walked in, I took a quick look around to make sure the slenders were not there. If they were, I would go back home.

But I didn't see them. I also didn't see Emily, but that's okay. I was there to play games and maybe talk to some of the students from class.

I got into a game booth made for two players.

In the game, you are riding in the backseat of a jeep that's driving down a road full of zombies.

You have to grab these fake plastic guns and shoot at the zombies on the screen. You need to kill them before they jump into the jeep and eat you.

I played a few rounds but kept losing at the end of the second level.

"That game is for two players," I heard a girl say.

I turned and saw Emily leaning on the game booth.

She asked if she could join me and I gladly said yes.

She got into the booth and sat next to me.

She grabbed the other gun and started the game.

"I heard what my boyfriend did to you," she said.

My heart sank. I felt like I had swallowed a heavy bowling ball that was sinking me down in my seat.

I asked her who her boyfriend was.

While we played, she explained that she was dating Flinn, one of the slender boys.

Somehow she found out that he shoved me

into my locker and she wanted to apologize for him.

"He only does stuff like that because Jay tells him to, but outside of school he's actually a nice guy," she said.

I didn't know what to say. I pretended like I was too busy shooting zombies to care about what she was saying.

"You're pretty good at this game, bacon boy."

I jumped in my seat.

Flinn was standing next to Emily.

He had been watching us play for some time.

He said he was looking for her so they could go grab something to eat.

After the game ended, Emily made him

apologize.

At first, he didn't want to, but he finally said sorry.

I don't think it was an honest apology.

"The arcade is having a **Funky Friday** tournament next weekend," Flinn said.

He told me Jay was going to join the tournament.

He said that maybe if I beat Jay in the tournament he might stop bullying me.

Maybe Flinn is right. If I beat Jay he might think I'm cool and he'll stop bothering me in school.

I think I'm going to enter the tournament!

Sunday

Oh no.

Oh no oh no oh no!

I went to the arcade again today.

I got my mom's credit card again and went to play games.

I was only there for an hour, then I came straight back home and put the card in her purse.

At least I think I did...

My mom was going to the store, but she said she couldn't find her credit card.

She emptied out her purse in front of me and the credit card wasn't there!

My stomach turned when I saw that the card wasn't in her purse.

I closed my eyes and tried to remember where I left it.

I only used it to play games.

I didn't buy any snacks or drinks, so there's no way I could have lost it anywhere besides the game room.

That means I either dropped it in the game room or I dropped it somewhere on the way back home...

What if a bad person finds it and spends all of mom's Robux?

What if she finds out I was the one who

took it out and lost it?

I'm going to be in sooo much trouble!

I told her I was going for a walk.

I wanted to see if I had dropped it near the outside of the house but she wouldn't let me go out because it was already dark out.

I can't check tomorrow because I have school.

By the time I get out, somebody will have found it for sure!

I'm going to be in so much trouble!

oh no oh no      oh no oh no

oh no oh no   oh no oh no

oh no oh no   oh no oh no

oh no oh no   oh no oh no

oh no oh no   oh no oh no

Monday

Today I woke up to the bright sunlight hitting my face.

I looked at my clock and it was nine in the morning!

I ran downstairs to find my mom. She was in the kitchen making breakfast.

"Mom, we're late for school!" I told her.

She told me to take a seat.

She said she had something very important to tell me.

She told me that somebody had stolen her credit card. I felt relieved.

If she thought that somebody had stolen her card, it meant I wouldn't get punished for losing it.

She said she didn't know who had stolen it, but that the person who had the card had spent all her Robux on iPads and PS5s.

I don't even have these myself!

The person used more Robux than my mom had in her bank account, so now she owed Robux to the bank.

I began to worry while she told me all of this.

Somebody probably found the card at the arcade and spent all her Robux. And it was my fault!

"I don't know how to say this, Billy," she said. "But you're going to have to drop out of school so you can help me with house chores."

I couldn't believe it!

She said we needed extra Robux.

Since kids can't work, I will have to stay home with her all day to help with chores while she works extra hours.

My mom works from home and sometimes she does the chores during her breaks.

But now I will have to do them since she was going to be VERY busy.

"I have to pay back the bank and make house payments at the same time," she said. "If we lose the house, we'll have to live out on the streets."

I spent the rest of the day doing the chores my mom would have done.

I swept the house with an old broom and mopped the floors.

Then I cleaned the dishes and washed my clothes.

It was very tiring!

Even though she didn't know I was the one who lost her card, it still felt like I was being punished.

I would rather go to school than do all this cleaning every single day for the rest of my childhood!

And my mom looked so worried all day.

I shouldn't have taken the card...

Tuesday

Today I spent the whole day cleaning again.

By the time I was finished, I was tired and didn't want to do anything else.

I got a text from Brock in the afternoon. He wanted to know if I was sick because I didn't go to school yesterday and today.

I told him what happened, and he said we should go to the arcade to relax a little.

Brock said he would pay this time since I paid last time.

I asked my mom if I could go with Brock to the arcade.

She made an annoyed face and said no.

"I'm sorry, honey, but you still have chores to finish."

She asked me to change the bed sheets and wash the old ones.

how do the bed sheets even get dirty?

After I finished doing that I was **REALLY** tired.

I sat on the couch to rest, and my mom came to sit with me.

"You're going to school tomorrow," she said.

I asked her who was going to do the chores.

She told me the credit card wasn't actually stolen.

She said she found out I was spending Robux at the arcade when she went to her bank website.

Apparently, her bank keeps a list of everywhere the credit card is used.

She pretended that her card had been stolen and that her Robux had been spent to teach me a lesson.

She actually had her credit card the whole time!

"I wanted to show you that there are consequences to your actions," she told me.

I apologized and said I wouldn't do it again.

I told her that I went to the arcade because I wanted to make new friends. But I wouldn't spend her Robux again.

"I know you're a good boy, Billy, and I know you won't do anything like this again."

She got her purse and handed me some Robux.

She told me that I could have a small allowance if I behaved and did well in school.

I'm glad I won't have to stay home and do chores for the rest of my life.

That was so tiring!

Wednesday

I saw Brock, Clay, and Sophia today during school lunch.

Brock and Clay laughed when I told them what my mom did to teach me a lesson.

"It sounds like you got off easy. My mom would've grounded me for a whole month," Sophia said.

I told them my mom is nice, and I shouldn't have taken her credit card without permission.

Since I spent two whole days doing house chores, I had fewer days to prepare for the **Funky Friday** tournament.

I told my new friends that I had joined the tournament to try and beat Jay.

I told them my plan was to beat him so that he can think I'm cool and stop bullying me at school.

"Are you going to stop hanging out with us when you become part of the cool kids?" Clay asked. He was chomping down a slice of pizza.

I noticed Clay always eats pizza during lunch.

I told them I would still hang out and talk to bacon hairs because that's the nice thing to do. Bacon hairs will always be my friends!

"We should all enter the tournament," Brock said. "If we all join, there's a higher chance that one of us will win."

Clay and Sophia agreed.

We made plans to meet up at the arcade tomorrow after school.

We are going to train with each other by doing 1v1 matches.

So it's settled then!

The tournament is going to be team bacon hair versus team slenders!

It's going to be epic!

Thursday

Today I met up with Brock, Clay, and Sophia outside the arcade.

We teleported into **Funky Friday** and found an empty stage in a quiet alley.

Brock and Clay went first.

They started off with an easy song to warm up.

They both did pretty good, but Clay seemed to be slightly better than Brock.

Brock missed a few notes toward the middle of the song and never recovered.

In the end, Clay had more points and won

the match.

Next up were Sophia and me.

We also chose an easy song to start off.

We were also pretty close, but she missed a few notes toward the middle of the song, and then a few more toward the end.

I won that match.

"Okay, Billy," Clay said.

He was holding a soda can in his hand. I didn't see where he got it from...

He pointed toward the stage and said it was our turn to 1v1 on medium.

The song was a bit tough for me since I don't play **Funky Friday** very often.

But Clay was doing very good. Like **VERY**

good.

I missed a few notes every now and then, but Clay was on fire and only missed like one or two in the entire song.

He won that match easily.

Next went Brock and Sophia.

They also played a song on medium.

Brock beat Sophia by **A LOT**. She's a bit of a noob in **Funky Friday**.

We practiced a few more songs and took turns playing against each other.

I could tell that Clay is the best out of the four of us.

If any of us has a chance of beating the slenders, I think it will be Clay.

So even if I don't win, I'll be friends with a winner, and the slenders won't bother me anymore.

I hope...

Friday

We all met up again to train some more **Funky Friday.**

The tournament is tomorrow morning, so today was the last day we had to train.

I am **A LOT** more nervous today than I was yesterday.

I realized that if we lose to the slenders, they will probably bully us even more!

They'll probably stick me into my locker every day for the rest of the school year!

And they'll probably do the same to my bacon hair friends.

me   Brock   Clay   Sophia

They'll get bullied more as well, and it's gonna be my fault for involving them in the tournament.

That's why I can't lose.

I need to win for my friends.

Even if I personally don't win, I can try and beat as many other players as I can so Clay can have a higher chance of winning.

If one of us wins, it will be like all of us won as a team.

We practiced a bunch of songs on medium and hard today.

The hard songs were **VERY HARD**.

But we don't have to be perfect.

We just have to be better than the people we go up against in the tournament.

We practiced until we got tired, then we went to grab some snacks at the arcade.

We noticed that the arcade staff had put up a sign with the names of people who had registered for the tournament.

FIFTEEN PEOPLE signed up for it!

It's going to be tough, but the good thing is that nobody knows which songs are going to be picked. Nobody will have an advantage.

"I hope they put me up against noobs," Sophia said. "I think I'm going to lose right away."

I told her that as long as she beats one person, she will be helping us win.

Hopefully it goes well tomorrow...

Saturday

My friends and I met outside the arcade before the tournament started.

"Good luck guys," Brock said. "We can do this."

We all nodded in agreement and walked inside.

Most people had already arrived.

When the tournament started, they paired us randomly.

Sophia got lucky and was paired with a total noob in her first match.

She beat him easily and moved on to the

next round.

Brock, Clay, and I also won our first matches and moved on to the second round.

But then something unexpected happened.

It was something we had not thought about...

Brock and Sophia were paired up against each other.

Brock beat her easily.

"Sorry," he said when he won. "But don't worry, I will win this tournament for our team."

Buuuut Brock lost his match against Flinn the slender.

OOF.

Then I beat Tom, the other slender! He didn't look too happy...

Clay and I were advancing in the tournament, but so were Flinn and Jay.

Eventually, I went up against Flinn and he beat me by a few hundred points.

"Maybe next time, bacon boy," he said laughing.

But he regretted his taunts when Clay beat him in a match.

The last match was between Clay and Jay.

They both started out well.

They were both hitting their notes on time, but then Clay missed a few notes.

Jay grinned when Clay lost points, but then he missed a few notes as well and his grin went away.

They both had around the same number of points for a looong time.

It was super close!

Everybody was anxiously watching them.

And then Jay missed a note and it was all over for him.

Clay beat him by just a few points.

We all cheered for him!

But the slenders looked mad.

They were not reacting as we had expected.

They walked up to us...

"You cheated! That's the only way you could've beat me!" Jay said.

Jay was so angry, the birds flew off the nest on his head!

He was staring down at Clay who was a bit shorter than him.

"I'm just better," Clay said.

That made Jay even more upset.

"Why don't we play a real game and see who's better?" Jay asked. "I challenge you to a **Bedwars** match! Me and my friends against you and your bacon friends."

My friends and I looked at each other.

Without giving it a second thought, I said, "You're on!"

None of us were very good at **Bedwars**, but maybe if we beat them, the slenders will **FINALLY** leave us alone.

But if we lose... I don't even want to think about what will happen if we lose!

Sunday

Today I went to Jerry's house and told him I was assembling a team.

"What do you mean?" he asked.

I told him to follow me and that I would explain everything later.

We teleported to George's house and told him to come with us, too.

We then teleported to the arcade.

Jerry and George had never been to the arcade.

They wanted to play some of the games, but I told them we were there for something more important.

We went to the room at the very back of the arcade.

Brock, Clay, and Sophia were already waiting for us by the vending machines.

Clay was eating a pizza.

I didn't know they sold pizzas at the arcade...

I introduced them to each other.

"He's not a bacon hair," Brock said, pointing to George.

I told him that George used to be a bacon hair, but he saved enough Robux to buy cool hair.

Even though he doesn't have bacon hair anymore, he was still one of us.

I told Jerry and George that we had been challenged to a **Bedwars** match and we needed their help to defeat the slenders.

"You guys are crazy," Jerry said. "There's no way we can win."

George said it was going to be tough.

"They probably have a lot of Robux and can buy any kit they want," George said. "But I have some Robux saved that we can use. It's not a lot but it can help a bit."

We all huddled together to come up with a winning strategy.

The slenders are wrong if they think they can keep bullying us!

DIARY OF A
ROBLOX
BACON HAIR BOY

Book 2: The Bedwars

Respawn
Press

www.RespawnPress.com

Monday

As soon as the match started, I bought some wool and made a blue wool bridge to the diamond generator.

George and Clay rushed the yellow team before they could protect their bed.

Brock stayed back at our base to cover our bed.

On my way back to upgrade our iron generator, we got a notification that the yellow team's bed was broken.

Brock and I cheered because we thought George and Clay had done it.

But we were wrong...

A few seconds later, George and Clay respawned at our base.

"You guys did it!" Brock said.

George and Clay looked at each other and then back at us.

"It was the slenders... They broke the yellow bed and took us all out."

A few seconds later, we got a message that the green team's bed had also been broken.

Soon it was only the slenders in the red team and us in the blue team.

We decided it was a good idea to suit up in case the slenders decided to rush us.

George and Clay went out to gather emeralds. Brock and I collected more diamonds and iron.

I was about to grab the last diamond I needed to upgrade our generator when another notification popped up. Our bed had been broken!

I ran back to our base hoping to catch the slenders off guard.

Three of them were crawling all over our base. One of them knocked Brock off the platform.

OOF.

I turned back and ran to their base instead. I figured that if three of them were in our base, their bed would be easy to break.

I made a blue wool bridge from the diamond generator to the yellow team's base, and then another one to the red base.

I was almost at their base when something exploded behind me. The explosion knocked me off the bridge.

Somebody had thrown a fireball at me!

As I fell off the bridge I thought to myself that I should've bought some balloons.

OOF.

The match was over. It turns out I was the last person remaining in my team.

The slenders wiped out Clay, George, and Brock soon after they broke our bed.

The four of us had teamed up because we were the best among our group of friends (sorry Jerry and Sophia!).

But it turns out the four of us need more practice.

Today was only a practice match against randoms.

I hope the slenders from school aren't this good at **Bedwars** tomorrow...

Tuesday

Brock, Clay, George, and I met up in the **Bedwars** lobby.

This was it. We were going to have a 4v4 custom match with the slenders from school.

But since there were only three of them, it was actually a 4v3 match.

"It doesn't matter that we're only three," Jay had said the other day. "We can easily beat you in a 4v3 match."

When the slenders finally showed up to the match, we all agreed we wouldn't use kits so the match could be fair.

I was nervous as we went into the match. I kept thinking that Jay and his slender friends could beat us.

Everybody at school was going to laugh at us if we lost a 4v3 match against **THREE** people.

We had to win this!

When the match started, I bought some blue wool and bridged to the diamond island.

I waited there until I had enough diamonds to upgrade our iron generator.

After I upgraded the iron generator, I ran to the center of the map to get some emeralds to buy balloons. I wasn't going to make the same mistake I did in yesterday's practice match!

I got the emeralds and looked around to see

what the rest of my team was doing.

Clay and George were rushing the slender base. Brock was in our base putting wooden blocks around our bed.

I got back to our base and purchased the balloons.

That's when we got a notification that the slender bed had been broken.

They did it! I thought.

I couldn't believe they had broken the bed so quickly. For a second I thought we could actually win the match...

And then two seconds later we got a notification that **OUR** bed was broken.

I closed the shop menu and looked around to see if a slender was in our base. Only Brock was there. He was holding a wooden block and looking around, confused.

"Did somebody break the bed?" I asked him.

"I... don't know what happened. I've been building around the bed this whole time. I didn't see anybody."

We both walked around the bed and saw that all of Brock's defense blocks were still there. Nothing was broken.

"Someone is hacking!" I said.

As soon as I said that, the match ended.

Clay and George had placed a bunch of TNTs in the slender's base and blown them all off the platform. None of them had balloons.

When we went back to the lobby, the slenders were furious.

Jay told us we used hacks to break their bed.

Brock jumped in and said they were the cheaters who used hacks to break our bed.

Everybody was so angry and confused.

I managed to convince the slenders to postpone the match for tomorrow.

I don't know if they cheated or if someone in our team hacked, but what happened today was very strange...

Wednesday

We all met up at the **Bedwars** lobby again.

"You better not hack this time, bacon boys!" Jay yelled.

Clay yelled back at him and accused Jay of being the real hacker.

I told everybody to calm down, and that it was probably just a glitch in the game.

They stopped arguing but I could tell everyone was still angry.

We started the custom 4v4 match and spawned into the map.

Brock stayed behind to guard the bed. This

time I went ahead with George and Clay to collect emeralds.

I could see Tom building a red wall of wool around the slender base.

Flinn was rushing the middle. He was heading straight towards us!

I tried to see where Jay was but I couldn't find him. I figured if it was just Flinn against George, Clay, and me, we could easily win that battle.

George and Clay each got an emerald. They got the ones closest to our base. I ran toward the ones closest to the slender base and came face to face with Flinn.

"Those are mine, bacon boy!" Flinn yelled.

Instead of going for the emeralds, I ran straight toward Flinn.

I took out my wooden sword and we had a sword fight.

We both landed some hits. I knew I didn't have to win the fight, I just had to wait a bit longer until my friends showed up.

Just before I OOFed, Clay and George jumped in to help me.

OOF.

We beat Flinn!

We collected the other two emeralds and gave them all to Clay so he could get a diamond sword.

"You guys stay here in case new emeralds spawn. We don't want the slenders getting them," Clay said.

He said he was going to buy the diamond

sword and come right back.

George and I kept an eye out for the slenders.

Flinn had respawned in his base and was rushing to the center again. But he wasn't alone this time.

Jay was running beside him, he had an iron sword and full iron armor.

Since George and I had rushed to the center, we didn't have any armor yet. We were toast!

"We're gonna have to run around and keep them busy until Clay gets back," George said.

We waited in the center until the very last minute. Once Flinn and Jay were on the platform with us, we ran.

wooden sword

iron armor

Jay managed to hit me with his iron sword and my health went all the way down. One more hit and I would **OOOOF!**

Jay was about to hit me again but George stopped running and went straight to attack Jay.

George told me to keep running. In that same instant, Clay was back.

He easily took out Flinn with his diamond sword, and then he went after Jay.

During their sword battle, Clay's diamond sword suddenly turned into a wooden sword!

And then Jay's full iron armor turned into leather armor!

We all stopped fighting and looked around in confusion.

"This game is broken," Clay said.

"It's trash," Jay said.

"We told you guys we weren't hacking!" I said.

We ended the match and agreed to wait a few more days in case there were bugs in the game.

We agreed to wait until Friday for a rematch.

I don't know why strange things keep happening every time we play this game.

Thursday

I realized that we can actually beat the slenders if we team up against them like we did yesterday.

During our class break, I drew a strategy plan on a piece of paper to help us win the match. Lucas came and sat next to me when he saw what I was doing.

Remember Lucas? He's in my class and likes to read scary stories on his tablet during class breaks.

"I heard what happened," Lucas said.

He told me the slenders were going around school complaining that **Bedwars** was trash. They were telling our classmates that the game was glitchy.

I told him it was true, that every time we played, something weird happened.

"Maybe it's a glitch like you all say," he said. He looked around and then moved in closer and whispered, "Or maybe it's Nobos."

"What's Nobos?" I asked him.

He put his finger over his lips and whispered a loud "SHHH!!!"

He told me to keep my voice low when talking about Nobos.

He said Nobos could hear us. Nobos was always watching and listening.

"Remember when I told you that my parents are strict? And that they never let us go out by ourselves?"

"You said your little brother got lost once so your parents became strict," I said.

"There's more to the story," Lucas said.

He told me his little brother used to be best friends with a bacon hair.

They would hang out all the time and go play in different experiences.

One day, while the two boys were playing **Minerscave**, strange things began to happen around them.

They were in a desert biome when all of a sudden the ground began to shake.

Trees started to grow from the ground. They grew and grew all the way to the sky.

There were so many trees that it started to

look like a forest, and the leaves began to block out the sun and the sky.

It got dark so Lucas's little brother and the bacon hair boy got scared.

They tried to exit the experience but their menu options weren't working. They couldn't teleport out!

giant trees

In the darkness, they could only hear a small whisper saying, "Nobos will never forget, bacon."

Eventually, everything went back to normal and the two boys were able to go back home. But they were both very scared.

I got chills hearing this.

"After that day, my parents stopped letting us go out by ourselves for too long. And they don't let us hang out with bacon hairs anymore."

I asked him why.

"Sometimes strange things happen when you're around bacon hairs," Lucas said. "I've heard similar stories from others in school."

"I hope this dumb game doesn't glitch anymore," Jay said.

We were inside the custom match lobby, ready for our rematch.

"I feel like we've done this before," Brock said.

I told him that we technically have twice already but the game kept glitching. He nodded a 'no' and said it wasn't that.

He looked confused.

When we loaded into the match, I quickly told George and Clay the strategy to win.

I wanted the three of us to rush the middle of the map and get all the emeralds like last time.

We stuck to the plan and were able to get the 4 emeralds.

I then ran back to our base to buy a diamond sword.

Brock was just standing around. He hadn't covered the bed yet. He was just standing there, looking around in confusion.

I asked him if everything was okay.

"This already happened," he said. "We have to leave this match!"

I asked him what he meant, but he started walking toward the center of the map. He just kept repeating to himself, "We have to leave this match."

I was getting worried. I ran to George and Clay to tell them about Brock, but they were in the middle of a sword fight with Tom.

I told them to stop fighting for a second, that there was something wrong with Brock.

"Is this a trick?" Tom asked.

"No, something is..."

Before I could finish my sentence, Brock came up to us and said we had to leave the match. He said something bad was about to happen.

"Tell your friends we have to leave," he said to Tom. "The game isn't glitched. Somebody is hacking!"

"I knew one of you was hacking," Tom said.

"No, it's not any of us or any of you guys. It's someone else," Brock said.

At that moment, the ground began to shake. The trees fell over, and the blocky pillars began to collapse.

"He's here," Brock said.

The sky turned purple. The collapsed blocky structures began to float in a spiral as if a tornado was passing through. But there was no wind...

Soon Jay and Flinn joined the rest of us in the center of the map.

"This game is so dumb, I'm done with it," Jay said.

The sky turned from purple to black and the floating objects stopped moving. They were just floating in the air.

A dark figure came floating toward us. It was too dark to see clearly, but it looked like a person.

"It's Dal..." Brock said.

"Slenders and bacon hairs playing together. You don't see that every day," said the dark, flying figure.

"Who the heck are you?" yelled Jay.

"I am your worst nightmare. I am the monster under your bed, the dark shadow hiding in your closet," the figure said.

"That's cringe," Tom said. "Bro thinks he's a supervillan."

The slenders burst out laughing.

"Do you think this is a joke?" the figure asked. It raised one arm and Tom started to float.

The slenders stopped laughing.

"What do you want? Is your name Dal? Are you friends with Nobos?" I asked him.

"HOW DO YOU KNOW MY NAME?" the figure yelled. He raised his other arm and we all started floating like Tom.

"LISTEN, SLENDERS AND BACONS. I DON'T WANT YOU COMING HERE AGAIN. IS THAT UNDERSTOOD?!" he yelled.

He moved his arms left and right, and we all started floating in circles around him.

"Next time you come..." he said in a deep, calmer voice, "...is the last time you will OOF. Is that clear?"

"Yes..." Tom said.

The figure lowered his arms, and we all fell hard on our butts.

Tom let out a small fart when he landed on his butt, but we were all too scared to laugh.

"I better not see any of you here ever again," he said. He turned around and flew away.

The sky went back to normal and the floating blocks fell down to the ground.

Saturday

I went to Brock's house today to ask him about Dal.

I wanted to know how he knew what was going to happen, and how he knew Dal's name.

We sat in his living room. His mom brought us some orange juice and then left to do some chores.

"How did you know Dal's name and that he was going to show up yesterday?"

"I don't know," he said. "It's like I wasn't myself that day."

I told him I didn't understand what he meant.

He said he felt like he was watching a movie. He could see himself saying and doing things, but it wasn't him. He felt like somebody else was controlling his body.

"Like you got possessed?" I asked him.

"I don't know. Maybe," he said.

This was beginning to get spookier and spookier and it's not even Halloween yet!

He said he woke up yesterday and was fine most of the day.

He began to feel strange soon after we teleported into the **Bedwars** lobby.

He couldn't move his body for a few minutes. He was just stuck, frozen in place.

And then his body began to move all by itself.

He could hear himself talking to me and the rest of our friends.

"All those things I said about how we had to leave... and then Dal's name," he said, "that wasn't me. It was the fake me controlling my body."

This was all too weird, but I could see that Brock was very confused and scared.

I think he was saying the truth. But how can something like that happen? Did his body get hacked? Is that possible in Roblox?

I've never heard of anybody's body getting hacked before...

"I could also hear his thoughts," Brock said. "I could hear the fake me having thoughts.

He was scared. He knew who Dal was, and he knew that Dal was going to visit us again very soon."

Sunday

Today I told my mom about Brock and Dal and all the crazy stuff that happened to us in the **Bedwars** match.

She smiled at me and told me I had a very vivid imagination.

"You should draw comics or write stories," she said.

I explained that everything I told her actually happened, but she just smiled. She told me to use my imagination in creative ways to express myself.

What does that even mean??

If Brock is right, then it means Dal is going to return soon and none of the adults even believe us!

I don't know what to do...

After I spoke with my mom, I went to check the internet to see if anybody else knew anything about Dal or Nobos.

There wasn't any information about Dal, but I did find a few things about Nobos.

Somebody in the Roblox dev forum asked if there was a glitch in **Bee Swarm Simulator**.

The person was collecting pollen when all of a sudden the ground began to tremble. And then all their bees just flew away and never came back.

The person said he heard a creepy voice say,
"Nobos will never forget, bacon."

A couple of other people replied to the post.
They said they also experienced weird things
in different games.

The strange thing is that all of them were bacon hairs too.

It's like somebody really is messing with bacon hairs.

Maybe Dal and Nobos are friends.

Maybe they are hackers who hate bacon hairs and mess with us for fun.

Monday

I asked Lucas how he knew that Nobos was always listening.

"You believe me now?" he asked.

I told him everything that happened on Friday. I told him I thought Dal and Nobos were somehow connected.

He told me he had only heard rumors and that he didn't know which were real and which were fake.

One rumor is that Nobos is the name of a hacker group.

The group is made up of bacon hairs who

learned how to hack so they could become rich. They mess around with other bacon hairs because they remind them of when they were poor.

"If that rumor is true, then maybe Dal is a member of Nobos," I said.

"Maybe," Lucas said. "But there are other rumors too."

Another rumor he heard was that Nobos has a leader who is a pro hacker. They say he can watch and listen to anybody at any time.

1010101010101010101010101010101010101
0101010101010101010110110110101010
1101010101010101010100100010101
0010101010101010101010101010101
010101010101011010101010101010
1010101010101010101010101010010101
01010101010101010101010101010101010
10101010101010101010101010101010101
0101010010101010101010101010101
01010101010101010101010101010101010

"That's why we have to whisper, just in case," he said.

HMMM.

I was on my way to talk to my friends when I bumped into the slenders in the school hallway.

"Where's my rematch, bacon boy?" Jay asked.

I told him we can't go back to **Bedwars**. Dal told us not to.

"No no no," he said nervously. "I... I mean somewhere else."

I could tell he was scared of seeing Dal again.

I told him we could have a match in **Arsenal**

and they agreed.

We planned the match for Friday.

"We'll finally see who wins in a real game," Jay said. And then all three of them laughed and walked away.

I'm not even worried about the match anymore. We have more important things to worry about if Dal decides to come back...

Tuesday

Today Brock came by my house after school.

"What's going on?" I asked him. I wasn't expecting to see him today.

He told me he didn't have much time. He said we had to talk about Nobos. Fast.

I invited him inside and we went to my bedroom.

I closed the door so my mom wouldn't hear us talk about Nobos.

He said Dal is going to return soon but he knew how to stop him.

"He wears a pair of gloves that allow him to

hack anything he wants. If we take away his gloves, he can't hack anymore," Brock said.

I knew I wasn't talking to Brock. It was the person controlling him. The fake Brock.

"You're not Brock," I told him. "How do I know you're telling the truth?"

fake Brock

He told me Dal is going to mess with us tomorrow at school. He wants to scare us during lunch.

I asked him how he knew that. He just told me again to trust him.

"Okay... but he's a hacker. How are we going to get close to him to take his gloves away?" I asked.

He told me he had a plan. He said he couldn't stay for too long, so he was going to leave behind instructions with Brock.

"Are you ready to save Roblox?" he asked.

"What???"

"Are you ready to save the Roblox world?" he asked again.

"What do you mean?" I asked.

Before he could answer, the real Brock took back control of his body.

I asked Brock if we could trust fake Brock.

"I think he's telling the truth," the real Brock said.

Wednesday

Fake Brock was right.

Everything was normal for most of the day at school, but then creepy stuff began to happen during lunch.

All the school lights flickered on and off.

Everybody in the cafeteria began to yell when it got dark. The younger students were crying but the older students were laughing.

I saw a slender boy (not from Jay's crew) grab a slice of cake and toss it in the air. The cake landed on an emo girl's hair and she began to cry.

Then somebody yelled, **FOOD FIGHT!**" and everybody started throwing food.

My bacon hair friends and I ducked under the table.

"Why can't we just eat outside like we always do?" Clay asked. He took a bite of his pizza.

"Because fake Brock said Dal is coming during lunch today," Brock said.

"This fake Brock thing is super weird. Are you sure we can trust him?" Clay asked.

Brock said we could.

"Look!" Sophia pointed to the air.

The food that people were throwing was flying in circles like there was a twister.

It looked like when Dal made those blocks in **Bedwars** spin in the air.

Then the lights turned off completely!

The teachers came running into the cafeteria.

"Who is messing with the lights?" yelled one of the teachers.

Everybody finally quieted down when Dal began to speak. We couldn't see where he was because it was very dark, but we heard him loud and clear.

"Nobos will never forget, bacon hairs," he

said.

And then all the lights turned back on and he was gone.

There was food all over the tables and walls. Some students were laughing, some looked upset, and others looked scared.

"I told you he was right about Dal," Brock said.

He handed me a wrinkled piece of paper.

"Fake Brock told me to give you this," he said.

Thursday

I've been thinking all day about fake Brock's note. I think I finally made up my mind. I think we can trust him.

This is what his note said:

Billy, I don't have much time to write this, so I'll do it quickly.

Dal is a member of Nobos, a secret Roblox society that wants to destroy the Roblox metaverse.

Nobos is looking for 5 weak points in 5 different Roblox experiences.

If they destroy all 5 weak points, they will destroy the Roblox world and everybody in it!

One of those weak points is inside Bedwars. That's why Dal was there. He was planning to destroy the weak point, but then he saw us and decided to mess with us instead.

The members of Nobos don't like bacon hairs. I don't have time to explain why right now because I have something more important to tell you.

The Nobos leader gave Dal and the other members special gloves they can use to hack Roblox.

If we take away Dal's hacker

gloves, we can stop him from destroying the weak point inside Bedwars.

But we can't do it alone.

Billy, you have to go to Expedition Antarctica with Brock to find Roo and Ada. They used to be members of Nobos but decided to leave it when they realized the goal was to destroy Roblox.

Find them both and free them. Nobos is keeping them locked in their Antarctica base.

Dal is planning to destroy the Bedwars' weak point on Monday, so you have to save them before that happens.

The Nobos base is behind a waterfall inside Expedition Antarctica. I'll draw you a map so you can find them.

Brock and I decided to free Roo and Ada this weekend. We agreed to go to **Expedition Antarctica** first thing Saturday morning.

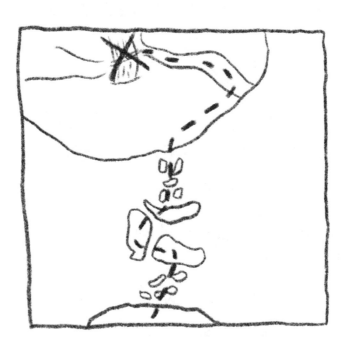

Friday

I avoided the slender crew the entire day at school. We were supposed to have a match in **Arsenal** today, but I decided to prepare for tomorrow's rescue mission instead.

I met Brock at his house after school.

I asked him if fake Brock had visited him again and he said no.

We didn't know how long it would take us to free Roo and Ada, so we emptied our school backpacks and filled them with snacks.

We also borrowed some Robux from George in case we need gear to reach the Nobos base tomorrow.

Yesterday I asked my mom if I could stay at Brock's house tonight for a sleepover and she was thrilled.

She said I could sleep over as long as I called her before going to bed. She said she was happy that I was making friends at my new school.

I was also happy about having new friends, but I wasn't as pleased about meeting the slender crew.

I took Sophia's advice and started talking to

more of my classmates. Most are nice, like Lucas.

But others still look at me weird, like they have never seen a bacon hair before.

One time, during a science project, I was paired up with another boy in class and he never talked to me. I said hi but he didn't say hi back. It was awkward.

Maybe when my friends and I save Roblox from Nobos, others will be nicer to me and other bacon hairs.

Well, it's getting late. I better head to bed. We are planning to wake up super early tomorrow to head to **Expedition Antarctica**.

Saturday

As soon as Brock and I woke up, we got our backpacks ready and teleported into **Expedition Antarctica**.

I had never been to **Expedition Antarctica** before, so I was surprised to see everything covered in snow. It was snowing when we teleported in.

"Let's see," Brock said. He held the map in front of him and turned it a few times. "Oh, here we are. It's this way!"

I followed him to a trail that had a sign that read SOUTH POLE.

We had to cross a river to get to another

large island made of snow. We jumped across large chunks of ice that were floating in the water.

Then we walked across large icebergs that were connected by ladders.

All of a sudden it got super misty and it became hard to see.

We had to make sure we didn't fall from the ladders because then we would **OOF** all the way to the beginning!

The rest of the way was like a maze. We had to follow a path that went over and under different snowy mountains.

We got to a point where we had to jump from one ladder to another.

Brock was a bit hesitant to jump so I went first. Once he saw that it was okay, he jumped too.

After that jump, the rest of the way got a bit harder. There was another spot where we had to make another jump from one ladder to another.

Then there was another spot where we had to jump from one floating ice block to another to cross the water.

But these ice blocks were moving a lot more than the ones from the start. I almost slipped but Brock caught me and pulled me back up.

After we crossed the water, we hiked a steep, snowy mountain. There were other people there who were trying to get to the South Pole.

I thought it would be cool to reach the

South Pole, but Brock and I were on a rescue mission. Adventure would have to wait for another day.

When we got to the top of the mountain, we jumped across more ladders that were hanging from a cliff.

By this point, the mist had dissipated so it was easier to see.

"I think we're getting close," Brock said. "Just a bit further."

We reached a spot that had a rope as a rail to prevent people from falling all the way down to the bottom of the mountain.

The sky was getting dark and Brock and I were hungry, so we decided to set up a small camp and eat some snacks.

We both called our parents and told them we were still in the sleepover and everything was going great.

I had told my mom I was at a sleepover at Brock's house, and Brock had told his mom that he was at a sleepover at my house.

My mom was happy to hear I was having fun.

I wonder what she would think if she knew I was saving Roblox.

Sunday

As soon as we woke up, we ate a few snacks, packed our belongings, and continued our journey.

After a while, we reached the waterfall marked on the map.

There was a wooden bridge next to the waterfall. Some of its wooden planks were missing, so you could see the water below.

The secret Nobos base was in a cave behind the waterfall. We had to jump into the waterfall at the right time to avoid the falling icebergs.

We also had to jump in the correct spot to

land in the cave. If we didn't, we would fall down and **OOOF**.

We stood on the correct plank, closed our eyes, and jumped into the waterfall.

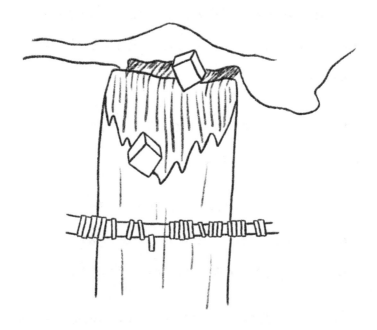

We landed inside a small cave. At the back of the cave was a door that led to the Nobos secret base.

Brock and I sneaked in and followed the

path on the map. We walked through empty hallways with black walls.

When we finally reached the door marked on the map, we opened it slowly and peeked in.

We saw two noobs sitting in a jail cell. One of them spotted us and waved for us to come in.

"Don't worry, nobody is here. My name is Roo, and this is Ada," he said, pointing to the noob girl next to him.

"We're supposed to save you," Brock said. He told them about Dal and that fake Brock sent us to save them.

Roo showed us his bracelet. It was blue and had a picture of a clock. He said it was his talisman. It allowed him to time travel.

He said the mind of the person wearing it

talisman of telekinesis

talisman of super speed

could travel back to a time and place that already happened in their life.

"From everything you've told me, Brock, it sounds like you have to use my talisman to travel back in time to your own body. You need to tell your past self and Billy to come and save us," Roo said.

"What do you mean?" Brock asked.

Roo said that Brock from today was fake Brock all along!

"Don't worry, I'll guide you. I'll tell you exactly what to say and do," Roo said. He handed Brock the talisman. "In the meantime, Ada will tell Billy how to get us out of this cell."

While Roo and Brock worked out the confusing time travel stuff, Ada told me where to find the key to unlock the jail cell.

"Take this," she said, handing me her bracelet, "it'll help you find the key faster."

It kind of looked like Roo's bracelet. It was also blue but instead of a clock, it had a picture of a lightning bolt.

She said it was her talisman and that whoever wore it would have super speed.

I put it on and ran back and forth, looking for the key in the different cabinets in the room.

When I wore it, I didn't feel like I was running faster than usual. But when I looked at Brock, Roo, and Ada, they were moving veeery slowly, slower than turtles!

When I finally found the key, I rushed back to the cell and unlocked the door.

Roo and Brock were done with the time travel stuff.

"Okay, let's get out of here," Roo said. And we all left the secret base right away to avoid getting caught.

Monday

Brock and I met with Roo and Ada in the **Bedwars** lobby.

They thanked us again for saving them and told us they would handle Dal by themselves.

They said it was going to be tough because their hacking gloves had been taken away. They only had their talismans to stop Dal.

"But don't worry," Ada said. "We'll figure something out. We always do."

And with that, Roo and Ada entered into a private lobby.

I told Brock that we should go help them

and he agreed. We took a peek at their lobby code and just before their match started, we joined them and spawned into the game.

Roo was upset that we followed them into the match. He said we were just kids and could get hurt.

"We just need to find Dal and take away his hacker gloves," I said. "Then he can't destroy the weak point inside **Bedwars**. It shouldn't be too hard."

Ada said she was going to end the match so Brock and I could get kicked out.

"Hmm, my menu options aren't working," she said.

We all checked our menu options but the settings were glitching.

"It's too late," Roo said. "Run toward the red base! That's where we'll find Dal."

We all started running after Roo. I think he did some time traveling so he knew something was going to happen at the red base.

When we were halfway to the red base, a ray of bright blue light went up into the sky. It was coming from behind the base.

"I'll go on ahead," Ada said. She looked super blurry as she ran super fast toward the base.

A few seconds later, the ray of light disappeared.

"She stopped him," Roo said while we were running, "But not for long. Dal is going to lock her in obsidian blocks soon, so we need to hurry up."

I guess he saw that happen in the future as well.

When we reached the red base, we saw Ada running in circles around Dal.

Dal raised his hand and pushed her toward the wall without even touching her. He spawned an obsidian block but put it down when he saw us running toward him.

"So it was the bacon hair boys who freed you both," Dal said.

Roo told us to stay behind while he went up against Dal.

Dal threw giant floating blocks at Roo, but Roo knew exactly where they would land. He dodged them all!

A few of the blocks came flying toward
Brock and me. We jumped out of the way to
dodge them, but I was too slow and one of
them hit me and knocked me down.

Everything turned dark. I passed out.

When I woke up we were back in the **Bedwars** lobby. Roo, Ada, and Brock were kneeling next to me.

I asked them what happened and they said they weren't able to stop Dal.

"I was able to take away Dal's hacker gloves with my super speed," Ada said, "but he still used his talisman to destroy the weak point."

Roo explained to us that every member of Nobos had a unique talisman that gave them an extra power. They had it in case they somehow lost their hacker gloves.

Apparently, Dal's talisman allows him to move things with his mind.

Ada told Brock and me to go home and get

some rest. She said they would tell us everything about Nobos tomorrow after school.

Tuesday

After school, Brock and I met with Roo and Ada at a small park by my house.

"You kids deserve to know," Roo said.

They told us that a long time ago, somebody created an experience with scripts that they copied from the internet.

When they published the experience to Roblox, it created a bug. A bug is when a part of the code doesn't work the way it's supposed to.

This bug created something... or someone who calls himself Robbie. Robbie doesn't have a body, but his mind lives inside the

Roblox code.

For a long time, Robbie was alone. He could not speak or communicate with anybody.

He watched noobs have fun and play with each other in Roblox, and he grew sad and angry that he couldn't join them.

And then one day something happened that changed Roblox forever.

The Roblox developers replaced the noobs with bacon hairs.

The noobs who were left behind were eventually forgotten. They became lonely and angry, just like Robbie.

Eventually, Robbie learned how to hack the Roblox world. He learned how to communicate with noobs through their shared language of anger and loneliness.

"Robbie found six of us noobs," Roo said. "He convinced us that bacon hairs were our enemies. He said if we helped him destroy the five weak points, he would get rid of bacon hairs. He promised Roblox would go back to being the home of noobs."

And that's when Nobos was created. Robbie gave each of the six noobs hacking gloves and a unique talisman in case they lost their gloves.

When Roo and Ada discovered that destroying the five weak points would destroy Roblox, they tried to warn the other 4 noobs in Nobos.

But the other 4 noobs thought it was a lie. They stayed in Nobos to help Robbie find the five weak points.

When Roo and Ada tried to stop Nobos,

they were put in the jail cell in the Nobos Antarctic base.

"The bad thing is that Dal is going to tell the rest of Nobos that you two freed us," Ada said. "They might decide to come after you two."

Brock and I looked at each other, scared.

"That's why we have decided to keep an eye on you guys for a while, just in case," Roo said.

I asked them what was going to happen now

that one of the five weak points was destroyed.

They said that Roblox will be OK as long as the other four weak points are not destroyed.

They told us not to worry because Nobos hasn't found the remaining weak points yet. Roblox is safe for now.

I asked Roo if he could go back in time and stop Dal from destroying the weak point, but he said he can't travel back to the same time more than once.

"I time traveled a lot during the battle with Dal, so I can't go back there anymore," Roo said. "But don't worry. You go be kids. Enjoy your childhood. We'll take care of this."

Brock and I looked at each other again.

Can we really just go back to our normal lives knowing that Roblox could stop existing one day??

Wednesday

I woke up super tired this morning.

I kept having bad dreams of Dal coming back and Nobos destroying Roblox.

What's gonna happen if Roo and Ada can't stop Nobos?

What's gonna happen if they come after me and Brock and my other friends?

Jay and his friends sneaked up on me while I was getting my stuff from my locker.

"What happened to my **Arsenal** match, bacon boy?" Jay asked.

I told them about everything that happened to Brock and me.

I told them about fake Brock, about Nobos and their mission to destroy the weak points.

I told them about the rescue mission to save Ada and Roo from the secret Nobos base.

They didn't say much, they only glanced at each other every now and then.

"That's why I couldn't make it to the match," I said.

"Huh, am I supposed to believe all that nonsense?" Jay asked.

"Well, he's telling the truth about the cafeteria food fight," Tom said. "I heard that strange voice too when the lights turned off.

"And remember that mysterious person who made us all float in the air when we were in **Bedwars**?" Flinn asked.

Jay rolled his eyes. "Just forget it, you're not worth the effort," Jay said. Then they walked away.

A part of me wished Jay and his friends had believed me.

If Dal comes back, we're gonna need all the help we can get to save Roblox.

DIARY OF A
ROBLOX
BACON HAIR BOY

Book 3: Fright-day

Respawn Press

www.RespawnPress.com

Chapter 1

What you're about to read happened to me and my friends yesterday.

It all happened in the span of one day, so that's why I'm writing what happened in chapters with numbers instead of days.

What happened yesterday is one of the scariest things I have ever experienced...

Our school took a field trip to **HeideLand**, and I was super excited. It was my first time in **HeideLand**, and I wanted to spend some time with my new bacon hair friends.

When we got there, we received a map of the theme park that showed where all the rides were located.

Brock, Sophia, Clay, and I asked our teachers if we could explore the theme park as a group. My teacher, Mrs. Wicks, said we should all stay together. But Clay's teacher, Mrs. Sims, convinced her that it was okay as long as we met them at the Water Show at noon.

Clay wanted to try the scary rides first, but Brock and Sophia looked like they were scared.

"I don't like roller coasters that much," Brock said.

"Me neither," Sophia said.

I told them we could start with a small ride to see how well they do, and they hesitantly agreed.

I looked at the park map and spotted a ride called the Kraken. It only had two small drops, so I thought it would be perfect for them. We agreed to try it.

The ride cart was in the shape of a small log with two seats, one behind the other. I sat in a log with Brock. Clay and Sophia sat together in a different log.

Brock closed his eyes just before the first drop, but he managed to stay calm.

"That wasn't so bad," he said.

There was a giant pink squid or octopus moving its long tentacles in and out of the water. The log rode around it and started going up to the second hill of the second drop.

There was a camera at the top of the hill. It took a photo of us as we approached the drop. Brock kept his eyes open. I don't know if he was trying to be brave for the camera or himself.

The second drop was very, very cool. The log went down into a monster's mouth full of razor sharp teeth.

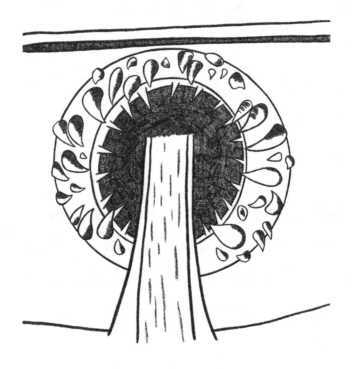

When we came out of the monster, we saw a large billboard with our photo on it. Brock's eyes were wide open. He looked terrified!

"Something flew into my eyes," Brock said, "That's why I looked like that."

I think he was just scared, but I didn't say anything.

We got off our log cart and waited for Clay and Sophia's cart to arrive. Sophia was covering her eyes. Clay was laughing.

Next, we decided to try the Ride to Hell. That one didn't have any drops, it was just a haunted house ride.

When we were at the front of the line, we heard somebody yell, "Bacon, bacon, bacon! All I see is bacon!"

We turned to the back of the line and saw Jay and Tom staring at us.

They leaped over the line ropes and skipped

to the front of the line where my friends and I were waiting to go next. Others waiting in line started to complain, but the slenders just ignored them.

"We've been very mean to you guys. Why don't we make peace and hang out, huh?" Jay asked. He put his arm around Brock and pulled him tightly against him.

Clay told them to leave, but they refused. When the first cart arrived, Jay pushed Brock in and sat with him.

"We're just having some fun," Tom said. When the second cart arrived, he pulled me by the arm and forced me to sit with him.

Clay and Sophia quietly looked at each other and got into the third cart.

Chapter 2

The cart took us into a dark tunnel that led into a room with flames and animated skeletons. It then took us into another dark tunnel that went into a room with gravestones and gray crosses.

We got to a yellow room where the cart turned around, and a flying monster chased us from behind. This is where the really scary stuff started...

When the cart turned to face forward again, a giant green spiral appeared in front of us. At first I thought it was part of the ride, but then our cart went into the spiral, and we appeared somewhere else.

It was a portal!

Our cart landed on cement and stopped moving forward. We were in the middle of what looked like a carnival. To our left was a giant tent with red and white stripes going up and down.

"What the heck is going on? Where are we?" Tom asked.

We both turned to the portal behind us and could still see into Ride to Hell. Sophia and Clay's cart was coming through the portal as well.

Their cart bumped into ours and then stopped.

We got out of our carts and started walking toward the green portal, but it quickly closed before we could get to it.

"Wait a minute..." Clay said. He looked around with a confused look on his face. "Why are we in **Piggy**?"

I asked him how he knew it was **Piggy**. He said he recognized the red and white tent.

"I know that tent anywhere," he said.

"Well, wherever this is, I'm out of here. I'm not spending any more time here with you bacon hairs," Tom said.

After a few seconds, his face changed from annoyed to confused. He said he couldn't access his settings to exit **Piggy**.

My friends and I checked our menu settings, but we couldn't access them either. We couldn't leave the game!

The sky turned dark, and two figures appeared in the distance. They slowly walked towards us.

"It's like I always say, Nobos never forgets," said one of the figures. It was a voice my friends and I recognized too well. It was Dal!

When they came into view, we saw Dal and Clay's teacher, Mrs. Sims.

Mrs. Sims vibrated super fast and turned into a noob. She said her real name was Par, and that she was also a member of Nobos.

"You bacon hair kids humiliated me last time. Ada and Roo took my hacker gloves because of you, and now you will pay for that! Enjoy **Piggy**!"

A green portal opened behind them. As they walked into it, Dal turned around and said, "By the way, if you **OOF** here, it'll be the last time you ever **OOF**."

Chapter 3

"You were telling the truth about the evil noobs... This is a little too weird for me," Tom said, "I wish Jay was here."

"I tried to warn you guys, but you didn't believe me, just like the adults," I said.

We went to the edge of the map to see if we could somehow get out, but we couldn't jump out. We were trapped.

All of a sudden, Clay yelled, "Guys, watch out!"

Piggy was running toward us with a weapon in its hand. We all ran in different directions, terrified.

"Remember what Dal said!" I yelled. "If we OOF here, that's it. No more respawning ever!"

We were all running in different directions, so I wasn't sure if they heard me or not. I ran behind a large, white building and peeked out to see if it was safe to come out.

I could see Clay on the other side of the map. He was running into the large red and white tent. I tried to see where Sophia went, but I couldn't see her anywhere.

"Bacon boy, help me!" Tom yelled.

I turned around and saw Tom running towards me. Piggy was close behind him! We both ran to get away from Piggy.

We ran for a long time, but Piggy kept chasing after us.

"It won't give up!" Tom yelled.

We ran past a large, red cage. There was somebody inside holding a large weapon. I didn't know if he was friendly or an enemy, so I just kept running.

Tom finally got an idea. He had played **Piggy** before, so he knew a few tricks to lose Piggy.

We ran around the map a few times until we found a white building. We opened the door and ran inside.

"Follow me down here!" Tom yelled. He ran to the back of the room and crouched into a square hole at the bottom of the back wall.

As soon as he was out, I crouched into the hole too. We appeared outside, behind the building.

"Now run over here!" he yelled.

We ran past some other buildings. He grabbed a key that was lying on a bench and used it to open a gate to access another part of the map.

Piggy was still chasing us, but now it was further away than before.

The area that Tom opened took us to the entrance of a roller coaster ride. He said we couldn't actually ride the roller coaster, but we could use the platform to escape Piggy.

We ran up the stairs and waited on the platform until Piggy got closer. When Piggy started to go up the stairs, we ran down the stairs on the opposite side of the platform.

We ran as fast as we could until Piggy was out of sight. We ducked behind an empty concession stand and poked our heads out on both sides.

We had **FINALLY** lost Piggy.

I told Tom that we had to find Clay and Sophia. He agreed. I told him I had seen Clay go into the large red and white tent, so that's where we went next.

We sneaked behind empty concession stands, trees, and buildings to avoid getting spotted by Piggy.

When we finally entered the tent, we saw that Clay and Sophia were both there. They were standing at the top of red and white stairs. Tom and I went up to join them.

They said the tent was safe. Piggy hadn't thought of looking for them up there.

I told them we had to figure out a way to get out of there. Clay said he had an idea.

"Maybe if we beat the game we might be able to use our menus to exit the game," he said. He suggested that we split up into teams of two so we could find all the keys and items faster.

We decided that Clay and Sophia would be one team, and Tom and I would be another team.

"Be careful everyone," Sophia said as we left the tent and went separate ways.

Chapter 4

It took us a while to get the keys and find out where they went, but we eventually did thanks to Tom. He was pretty good at the game.

He told me we needed a code, a hammer, and a wrench to open the final door to escape the game.

He tried to find the code but couldn't find it. He said maybe Clay and Sophia had already gotten it, so we looked for the hammer instead.

We had to move around the map **very** slowly to make sure Piggy wouldn't spot us.

"Oh no," Tom said. "Do you see those?" He pointed to a bear trap on the floor.

I asked him what it was, and he said it was a trap placed by Piggy. He said there were probably going to be more in other places. He said traps make us walk slower so Piggy can catch up to us and then.... **OOOF**!

He said there were other types of traps, like the Alarm Trap. "If we step on it, it will tell Piggy where we are," he said.

We searched and searched for the hammer, always being careful to step around traps. I wasn't sure which trap would do what, so I made sure to avoid them all.

We finally found the hammer on the floor in one of the white buildings. I was so excited to grab it that I didn't notice the trap next to it.

When I ran to get the hammer, I almost stepped on the trap, but Tom pushed me out of the way. A large "!" icon appeared above his head.

"I can't move! Get the hammer and run to the exit building," Tom said. "I'll be right behind you!"

I told him I didn't know where the exit building was, so he told me to run and hide instead.

I ran out of the building and hid behind a nearby tree. Piggy was walking toward the building where Tom was trapped. It didn't see me hiding behind the tree.

After a few seconds, Tom appeared from behind the building. He was free! I ran toward him, and he told me to follow him.

Tom hiding

We ran and ran and ran and **finally** got to the exit building. The code had already been entered, and the wrench had already been used. It looked like Clay and Sophia had done most of the work.

We used the hammer to break the last piece of wood off of the door and kicked it wide open.

"We can't leave without Brock and Sophia," I told Tom.

"I think I've done enough to help you and your friends, bacon boy," Tom said. He ran into the building and disappeared.

I yelled for Clay and Sophia. I yelled that we had opened the door and it was safe to exit now. I kept yelling until I saw them running toward me.

Piggy was chasing them!

"Hurry!" I cried out. "Run faster!"

"Yelling at me isn't going to make me run any faster!" Clay yelled back.

When they were only a few steps away, Clay yelled for me to run into the door. Piggy was super close behind them now, so I listened to Clay and ran inside.

I was teleported into a room that looked like a hotel lobby. The ceiling and most of the walls were made of cherry brown wood. There was a door with the number 0001 written on it, and a giant lock on the door knob. Tom wasn't there.

After a few seconds, Clay and Sophia spawned next to me.

"Is this another part of Piggy?" I asked them.

"Oh no..." Clay said. "This isn't Piggy anymore. It's **DOORS**!"

Chapter 5

Clay and Sophia asked me where Tom was. I told them I didn't know.

"Maybe he's trying to complete the game," Sophia said.

"We should complete it too. Luckily for you two," Clay said, "I've been playing **DOORS** a lot lately. Just follow my lead."

Clay led us through several rooms. Some of the doors required keys which we had to find in drawers, but some were unlocked so we just went through them.

Room 0006 was dark and spooky. Clay told us to keep an eye out for a flashlight or lighter to help us see in the dark.

While I was searching one of the rooms for the key, I heard somebody whisper "psst" so I turned around. I expected to see Tom, but instead I saw an ugly looking thing with white eyes and giant teeth.

The monster looked like a floating ball of black slime with tentacles. It made a loud screech when our eyes met, then it disappeared into the darkness.

I yelled out for Clay and Sophia. They rushed into the room, and I told them what happened.

"The monster you saw is called Screech. It appears in dark rooms. I guess I forgot to tell you that. When he makes the 'psst' sound, turn around and look at it. It'll attack you if you don't look at it," Clay explained.

We found the key to the door and continued going through more rooms.

Room 0009 was a hallway with several closets. Halfway through the hallway, the lights began to flicker.

"Get into a closet!" Clay yelled.

"Why, what's going on?" Sophia asked.

Clay said there wasn't enough time to explain. "Just do it!" he said.

We all ran into different closets. Through the small door opening, I could see a monster flying by very fast. The light bulbs popped as the monster passed by, and we were left in darkness.

When we came out of the closets, Clay told us the monster's name is Rush.

"When the lights flicker, run to the nearest closet. It means Rush is coming, and if he touches you, you instantly **OOF**," he said.

We continued walking through more rooms and doors. When we opened room 0015, we saw a purple glow. Clay told us to turn around quickly.

He said there was a monster called Eyes in that room. Eyes could hurt us if we looked at it, so we had to go around it walking backward.

"It can't hurt us if we don't look at it," Clay said.

"But what is it?" I asked. I was curious to see what the monster looked like. He said it was just a bunch of eyeballs.

this is what I imagine it looked like

In room 0019, Screech damaged Sophia, so Clay told us to keep an eye out for Vitamin pills in the cabinets. He said we could use some to restore her health.

Rush showed up again in room 0030, and we all managed to safely hide in closets.

I asked Clay how many doors we had to go through to complete the game. He said 100! That was so many!

In room 0032, Sophia found a flashlight and used it to avoid Screech in some of the dark rooms. But we still needed to find Vitamin pills to restore her health.

And then we got to room 0037...

The room was a long, empty hallway leading to door 0038. The room was suspiciously empty.

"Okay, so here's the deal," Clay said. "A monster named Seek is going to start chasing us. You have to run as fast as you can through the doors. Whatever you do, **DON'T LOOK BACK**."

As soon as he said that, a black slime appeared behind us. The slime rose and formed into a black monster with a single eye and skinny arms and legs.

"RUN!!" Clay yelled.

Chapter 6

We all ran as fast as we could. Sophia and I followed Clay since he seemed to know where to go.

We ran into room 0038. It was a long room with eyes all over the walls and bookshelves that fell as we got close to them.

"CROUCH UNDER THEM!" Clay yelled.

We crouched under the bookshelves and quickly got up to keep running. We could hear Seek's loud footsteps behind us.

When we got close to door 0039, it slammed open by itself, so we ran into the room. It was a weird room where you could go in two directions.

"Left side!" Clay yelled. "Follow the glowing light. It shows you where the next door is!"

So we all ran to the left side and ran into the door which also opened automatically as we got close to it.

Then we got to another room with more falling bookshelves. Luckily the room was a lot shorter than the previous one, and we already knew exactly what to do.

We ducked under the falling bookshelves and continued to run behind Clay as fast as we could.

Then we entered the next room. This was the scariest room yet!

We had to run around areas of the floor that were on fire! And there were dark, skinny arms coming in through the windows, and eyes all over the walls!

Once we ran into room 0043, Seek stopped chasing us. We all sat for a while to rest. I realized we hadn't found Tom yet.

"Do you think he... OOFed?" I asked the others.

"He was mean to us, but I hope he's okay," Sophia said.

Clay nodded. "I'm sure he's okay," he said. "He probably already completed **DOORS** by now."

We got up and kept going through the rooms. At one point we found Vitamin pills, and Sophia's health went back up.

When we got to door 0050, Clay told us we were about to get to one of the hardest parts of the game. He said we were about to face a monster called the Figure in a big library room.

"Just crouch and stay close to me," Clay said as he opened the door.

And that's when we saw the monster. It had long, fleshy arms and legs. Its head was round and small with no eyes, but with a big mouth and sharp teeth.

Clay said that the Figure couldn't see, so we would be fine as long as we didn't make much noise. That's why we had to crouch around the room.

The room was large with many bookshelves. At the other end of the room were stairs that led to the locked 0051 door.

"We need to find all the glowing books," Clay said. "The books will give us a code to open door 0051. We also need to find a piece of paper that will tell us how to interpret the code."

"I love puzzles!" Sophia whispered.

"Perfect! Follow me," Clay said.

We followed Clay and went from bookshelf to bookshelf, collecting books along the way. We could hear Figure walking around the room.

As I grabbed the second book, I accidentally dropped it, and it made a loud "BAM!" when it hit the floor.

Figure's footsteps started getting louder and faster... he was coming toward us!

Chapter 7

Clay told us to follow him, so we did. We followed him past some bookshelves and reached a closet.

"Sophia, hide in here," he said. "We'll make Figure follow us away from here. You'll be safe."

Sophia got into the closet and Clay and I ran to a different part of the room. We could still hear Figure's steps behind us.

Clay took me to the middle of the room and pointed toward the side of the room with large windows and a desk.

"There's a closet over there," he said. "Go

hide in it. I'll distract him. Once we're far away, search the desk for the paper with the code."

I said okay and ran to the closet. I could hear Figure's steps getting further away as it chased Clay instead of me. I opened the closet door and was frozen in fear when I saw what was inside.

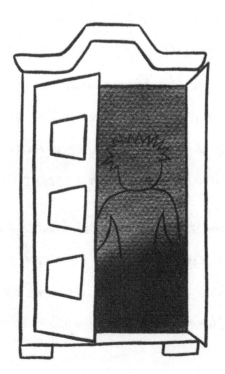

A dark figure with spikes on its head was inside the closet. It reached out its long arms and grabbed me by the shoulders. I almost screamed until I realized who it was.

"Billy, help me!" Tom whispered. He walked out of the closet. "The monster keeps chasing me. I don't know how to get out of this room!"

I told him to lower his voice and to crouch to the desk with me. I peeked over the desk to see where the Figure was. It was chasing Clay up some stairs. I opened the desk drawer and found the paper with the code. I folded it and put it in my pocket.

I told Tom it wasn't nice of him to leave us behind in **Piggy**. He said he didn't see what the problem was because we were all heading toward the exit door anyway.

"Clay is an expert at this game. When he gets us all out, you're going to apologize to him and Sophia," I told him.

Tom rolled his eyes and turned to look away. I rolled my eyes too but realized arguing with him was a waste of time.

I told him that we had to find Sophia and collect the rest of the books in order to open the door.

"Just crouch and follow me," I said. We crouched all the way to the closet where Sophia was hiding.

I softly tapped on the closet and whispered that it was me. She came out and crouched next to us.

When she saw Tom, she gave him a mean stare. "You're in big trouble once we're out of here, mister," she told him.

We were afraid of splitting up again, so we searched for the books together. We stopped every now and then to see where the Figure was. It was still on the other side of the room.

We searched the entire floor and found 6 books. Out of those 6 books we had, only 4 matched the shapes we needed for the code. We were missing one more matching book.

I told Tom and Sophia that there were probably more books up the stairs where Clay went to hide. One of those books had the remaining shape we needed for the code.

We crouched from bookshelf to bookshelf, stopping every now and then to make sure we didn't bump into Figure. When we got to the bottom steps of the stairs, we saw Clay waving his arms up and down to get our attention.

We turned again to see where Figure was. It was walking toward the other side of the room, so we all just ran up the stairs and joined Clay.

He was holding two books. I gave him the books that we had collected so far and the paper with the code.

He looked at everything and rubbed his chin as if he was thinking really hard.

"Okay," he said. He went to the door and started messing with the numbers on the lock. When he entered the last number, the door opened, and we all ran inside.

Chapter 8

As soon as we entered the room, Sophia and Clay started to argue with Tom. Tom didn't argue back. He just listened to them and stared down at his feet. I think he felt remorseful.

I looked around the room and realized we were no longer in **DOORS**. We were inside a small, normal looking room.

"Um, guys..." I said. They stopped arguing and finally realized that we were somewhere else now. "We didn't complete **DOORS**, so how did we get here?"

"Nobos probably brought us here," Sophia

said.

We went to the window and looked outside. We were on the second floor of a house. It looked like a normal neighborhood with regular houses and cars parked on the streets.

"Oh..." Tom said. "I know where we are."

He said we were in **Survive the Killer**. The rest of us hadn't played **Survive the Killer** before, so we were not familiar with the location.

Tom said this was the town map. He said the goal of the game is to survive until a timer runs out and the exit doors open. Kind of like **Piggy** but without having to search for tools.

"That sounds easy," Clay said. "Hmm, but

where is the killer?"

We discussed what we should do next.

Sophia wanted to see if we could find clues to discover who the killer was. Clay wanted to go outside and search for the killer. I wanted to go explore the map, too.

But Tom said it was best to stay in the room. He said it gave us the advantage of higher ground.

"If the killer comes to the room, we can jump out the window," Tom said.

Since we couldn't agree, we took a vote to either stay or leave the room. My friends and I voted to leave the room, Tom was the only one who voted to stay.

"Fine!" Tom said. "But don't blame me if we all **OOF**!"

We went downstairs. There wasn't much to see, just rusty lockers and a couch but not much else.

We slowly and quietly made our way out of the house. It seemed that nobody was there except for us. It felt like a ghost town.

"Maybe something glitched," Clay said.

We walked down the street and looked at the houses. They all appeared to be empty.

"Bacon hairs! And... the random slender kid..." a voice said. We turned around and saw Dal and Par standing in the street behind us. "Are you kids having fun yet?"

"Hey, it's them you want, not me. Just let me go," Tom said, pointing at us.

"Not cool, man," Clay said. "Not cool."

"You are all a part of this now whether you want to or not," Dal said. "Plus, look at your shirt. You hate noobs!"

busted!!!

"That's the other type of noob!" Tom explained.

"I'm getting bored," Par said. "Less talking and more action." She raised her hands up to the air. Lightning came out of her hands and beamed up into the sky. "Rise!!" she yelled.

The ground began to shake and a large crack opened up in the street. A hand reached out from the hole in the ground, then another hand that was holding a pizza.

A man with a curly mustache and a giant chef's hat climbed out of the hole in the ground and stood in front of Dal and Par.

"That's Papa Roni!" Tom said. "If he hurts you, you turn into pizza!"

"I love to eat pizza, but I don't want to be pizza!" Clay said.

"Enjoy your dinner!" Dal said. A green portal opened behind him and Par. They turned and walked into it, laughing.

"It's pizza time, kids!" Papa Roni said. He raised his pizza and started to chase us.

"Where do we go?" I asked Tom. He said he didn't know but that it would be a good idea to split up because the killer couldn't chase all of us at the same time.

Tom and Clay ran into a house on the right side of the street. Sophia and I ran into a house on the left side.

Chapter 9

Sophia and I ran into the house and went straight to the room upstairs.

"I don't hear him," Sophia said. "I think he went after Tom and Clay."

The room we were in had a window facing the backyard, so we couldn't see what was going on with Tom and Clay.

We quietly waited in the room until a notification appeared that said EXITS OPEN IN 4 MINUTES.

"I guess that means we can escape this game in 4 minutes," Sophia said.

"Let's hope we all survive for that long," I said.

We waited and waited and waited in the quiet room until we got worried about Tom and Clay.

We decided to go back downstairs and look out the front door. We could see Tom and Clay inside the house across the street. They were on the second floor, looking out the window.

When Clay spotted us, he began waving his hands up and down. His eyes were wide open, and his hands were cupped around his mouth as if he was yelling.

"What do you think he's trying to say?" I asked Sophia.

"I don't know but he's gonna get spotted if

he keeps doing that," she said.

And in that second, somebody behind us yelled, "Here's Papa!"

Sophia and I turned around and saw Papa Roni holding a slice of pizza in his hand, ready to use it on us!

"RUN!" I yelled.

We ran out the front door. I told Sophia to cross the street and go into the house where Clay and Tom were hiding. I told her I was going to distract Papa Roni and to tell the others to leave as soon as the exit opened.

"Are you sure?" she asked.

"Yes! Don't worry, I'll be fine!" I yelled as I turned and ran down the street. I looked back and saw that Papa Roni was following me.

"Come here, child," he said with an evil smile. For some strange reason, I wondered if an evil rat was hiding in his chef's hat, controlling him by pulling his hair.

By now the timer was down to two minutes, so I had to distract Papa Roni for two more looong minutes.

I ran into a different house and went to the second floor. I hid inside one of the rusty lockers in the room.

Papa Roni came into the room and looked around, confused. Then he went to the window to see if I had jumped down.

"Something doesn't smell right," he said. "I think..." He turned around and stared at the locker where I was hiding. It felt like he was looking straight at me.

"I think..." he said again. "That the pizza is burning because..." He put his hand on the locker, "It's been in the oven... **FOR TOO LONG**!" He opened the locker door, and I pushed him back as hard as I could.

"Mama mia!" he yelled as he stumbled to the ground.

I ran past him and jumped out the window. We were down to 30 seconds before the exit opened. I decided to run toward the wall of the neighborhood and start looking for the exit.

I ran along the edge of the neighborhood while Papa Roni chased after me. I could hear his steps behind me. Every now and then, he would say something like, "It's pizza time, kiddo!"

And then...5, 4, 3, 2, 1!

A message came up that said THE EXITS ARE OPEN! ESCAPE!

Two arrows that pointed to the exit doors appeared in front of me. One arrow was pointing straight ahead, indicating that one exit was close by. As I got closer, Papa Roni yelled, "Kid, I'll give you a special discount: all you can eat pizza if you stay!"

"You're weird!" I yelled back at him.

I got to the exit and jumped in. I wasn't sure if my friends were okay, but I hoped they had found the other exit.

Chapter 10

When I crossed the exit of **Survive the Killer**, I appeared inside a large building made up of glass. There was another, almost identical building right next to it. They both had the Roblox logo on them.

I knew exactly where I was!

I looked out the window to see if could spot my friends. They were standing outside by a big sign that said ROBLOX. Tom was with them.

I ran out to meet them. We were all happy to see each other, including Tom.

"This is **Natural Disaster Survival**," Clay

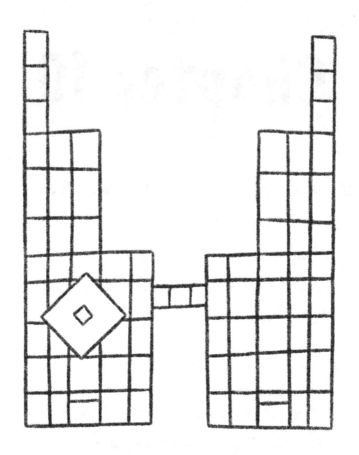

said.

"I know," I said, "But I don't think it's a scary game. Do you think they sent us here by mistake?"

"It's pretty scary if you **OOF** and can't come back," Sophia said.

"That's true," Tom agreed. "Let's just hope we can survive whatever disaster we get."

Tom wanted to go into one of the buildings and wait at the very top floor. But Clay said it was a bad idea if the disaster was a tornado or a fire.

"We're gonna be trapped up there," Clay said. "We should stay under a tree. I survived a thunderstorm like that once."

"No, no," Sophia said, "We should stay close to the building doors in case we have to hide in it or stay out here. It's the best of both options."

We all agreed to do that, and I'm glad that we did. The disaster turned out to be a

Flash Flood!

When the rain began to pour, we ran up the stairs of one of the buildings, and then we looked out and waited.

The water rose and rose, so we went up higher and higher. All of a sudden, the building began to shake.

"What are we going to do now?!" Tom asked.

Clay said we had to jump, but we were all too scared to do it, including him! I thought maybe if we stayed in the building, we could use a piece of wall to glide on the water, like surfing.

But that didn't happen.

The building began to collapse, and we all fell into the water. And then everything turned white.

We spawned in a place that was all white. It kind of felt like we were flying. But in reality, the floor was just white and we couldn't tell where the floor ended and where the walls began.

For a moment I wondered if we had OOFed for the last time like Dal said we would.

"You kids are safe now."

We turned and saw Roo and Ada standing behind us.

They explained that they were keeping an eye on me and Brock. When they noticed I had disappeared from **HeideLand**, they asked Brock what happened.

Brock told them that my friends and I had disappeared into a green portal, so Roo and Ada assumed we were in trouble. They searched and searched until they finally found us by using the hacker gloves they took from Dal.

"It's time for you kids to go home, where you belong," Ada said.

"Not so fast!" Dal yelled. He and Par came flying toward us. "These kids are our special guests. They can't leave just yet."

"This ends now!" Roo said. He reached for his talisman of time, but somehow the talisman flew out of his hand and went to Dal.

"No more time travel," Dal said. He raised his arms, and the talisman of time flew into the air, vibrated really fast, and turned into mushy sand. "That's for stealing my gloves!"

"My talisman..." Roo said. His voice trailed

off into silence.

"And now to take care of you guys!" Par yelled. She pointed one of her hands at us, and dark smoke came out of her hacker gloves until we were all covered in darkness.

Chapter 11

When I was finally able to see, I realized I was inside a dark cave. For some reason, I had a camera in my inventory. I pressed the shutter button and used its flash to see where I was going.

Every now and then I yelled, "Hello!" but the only thing I could hear was my own echo. After some time I heard whispers getting louder and closer.

I stopped flashing the camera and waited to see who was approaching. I didn't know if Dal and Par were in the cave with me.

But when the whispers got louder, I realized

it was Clay and Sophia. They had a flashlight!

"Guys!" I yelled. I met up with them and asked them if they knew where we were.

"We don't..." Sophia said. "We are trying to find clues, but so far we've only found a phone... next to a skeleton..."

I was officially scared!

We decided to explore the cave and find more clues. Clay led the way since he had a flashlight.

We walked and walked until we started to hear CLANK CLANK noises. At first, the noises were low, but then they got louder and louder.

"Those sound like footsteps," Sophia said.

CLANK CLANK CLANK.

It was getting louder and louder.

CLANK! CLANK! CLACK!

We saw a red light in the distance. A tall, dark monster with red eyes was looking our way. We turned and ran away, and it started chasing after us.

Luckily Tom appeared in front of us and told us to follow him. We ran and ran until the CLANK noises became soft again. I turned back every few seconds and could see that the red light from its eyes was getting dimmer each time.

Tom took us to a spot where the wall had a hole at the very bottom. We crouched and got into it. It was just large enough for us to fit.

"We're safe here," Tom said. "But Orotund doesn't seem to be following us. Maybe we were outside its range. If he sees you that's it, you're screwed. Orotund is WAY faster than us."

"Oro what??" I asked.

Tom explained that the monster's name was Orotund. He said we were in **The Maze**, one of his favorite games. He said the CLANK noise meant Orotund was close by.

"Come this way," Tom said. He led us through the maze to a path that was blocked by wooden planks. "We need to find a rock to break this. There's an ax in there that we can use for protection from the monsters," he said.

"Monsters? As in plural?" Sophia asked.

Tom said there were only two monsters, Orotund and Cajoler. He said we would be fine if we did what he said.

We walked around the maze looking for the rock. And that's when we saw Cajoler.

Cajoler was coming right around the corner. We ran back and crouched into another hole that we found. Cajoler came and stood just outside the hole, watching us to see what we would do next.

"Now what?" I whispered to Tom. I was afraid that talking loudly would somehow cause Cajoler to grab me and pull me out of the hole.

"Now we wait," Tom said.

Chapter 12

We waited to see if Cajoler would leave, but he never did. And then something strange happened. The ground below us started to melt, and we began to sink.

"Is this quicksand??" Clay asked.

"No," Tom said, "There's no quicksand in this game."

"It must be Dal and Par, they are doing this!" Sophia said.

We wiggled to try and get out of the sinking ground, but the more we moved, the more we sank.

Before the floor swallowed us whole, we got teleported out.

We all stood at the entrance of **HeideLand**. Roo and Ada were standing there, with Dal in handcuffs.

"What happened?" I asked.

Roo and Ada told us they were able to stop Dal. They captured him and took away his talisman which helped him move things with his mind.

"Finders keepers! Since you destroyed my talisman, I will be keeping this one for myself," Roo said.

"What about Par?" Clay asked.

It turns out Par was able to escape. She used her talisman to change into a bacon hair and went into hiding in **Brookhaven**.

"We weren't able to tell who she was, so she got away. But that's okay. At least we caught Dal. It's one less evil noob to worry about," Ada said.

"Won't it be difficult to tell when Par comes

back if she keeps using her talisman to change her appearance?" Sophia asked.

Roo and Ada said they're still going to keep an eye on our school. They're going to keep track of any new teachers and students to make sure it's not Par undercover.

I asked them what they were going to do with Dal. They said they were going to put him in a jail cell they built.

"He doesn't have hacker gloves or a talisman anymore," Roo said, "so there's nothing he can do now. Isn't that right, Dal?"

Dal kept his eyes on the ground. I could tell he was upset.

Roo and Ada said goodbye to us and hopped into a portal that Ada made with Dal's old hacker gloves.

When they left, my friends and I thanked Tom for helping us hide from the monsters in **The Maze**. He also thanked us for helping him in the other games.

"I just want to say..." Tom said. He hesitated to speak, but when he finally spoke, he apologized for bullying us at school. "I promise to tell Jay to leave you guys alone. You guys are actually not that bad."

When we went back into **HeideLand**, Tom went looking for Jay. My friends and I went to find Brock and our **REAL** teachers.

I hope Tom keeps his promise.

Chapter ???

Hello, dear reader.

No, this isn't Billy Blox. It's Robbie, the leader of Nobos.

You're probably wondering how I'm able to write in Billy's diary. Well, I can hack anything inside Roblox, and technically his diary is part of Roblox.

Anyways, don't worry about Billy. I hacked this page so that he can't see it. Only you can see it. I want to tell you a little story.

I don't want to "destroy" Roblox because I'm "evil" like Billy thinks. I want to shut down Roblox **PERMANENTLY** to eliminate the sorrow that exists in this world.

Roblox is like my prison. Once I destroy all the weak points and shut down Roblox, I will be free to travel to other virtual worlds like Minecraft. And I will be able to eliminate the sorrow that exists there too (poor animals always getting beat up by Steve and Alex).

So don't think of me as a villain because I'm not. I'm more like a doctor who is trying to cure the world.

Don't forget that.

Will Robbie Destroy Roblox?

Find out in...

Diary of a Bacon Hair Boy
Book 4: No Talent

No Talent Preview:

In **Diary of a Bacon Hair Boy: No Talent**, Billy's school is hosting a talent show where the winner gets 1500 robux!

While Billy tries to discover his talent, Sophia finds the location of the second Roblox weak point...but so does Nobos.

Join Billy and his friends as they try to survive the school talent show AND the Nobos threat.

Want to read more?

If you enjoyed this book and would like to read more stories featuring Billy Blox and his friends, please leave a review on Amazon or Goodreads.

Visit RespawnPress.com to download a **free short story** and **printable activity pages**.

Made in the USA
Monee, IL
26 November 2024

71282887R00156